Lario Sinigaglia

English: the she language of Virginia Woolf

Youcanprint *Self-Publishing*

Title | English: the she language of Virginia Woolf
Author | Lario Sinigaglia
ISBN | 978-88-92677-62-3

Youcanprint *Self-Publishing*
Via Roma, 73 - 73039 Tricase (LE) - Italy
www.youcanprint.it
info@youcanprint.it
Facebook: facebook.com/youcanprint.it
Twitter: twitter.com/youcanprintit

CONTENTS

PREFACE

I begin with the hypothesis that there are female types of psyche and male types of psyche and conclude that there are "male languages" and "female languages". In these terms, the English language is considered to be "female", while the main languages of the European continent are "male".

The section of this book dealing with psychology is based on *Psychological Types,* the extensive volume by C.G. Jung whose findings I summarise in the first chapter.

The section concerned with linguistics is based on the works of Virginia Woolf, whom I consider to be a great commentator on the psychology of the English language.

In the second chapter, I discuss the sociological investigation of womanhood that forms a key component of Woolf's *Three Guineas* (all quotations are from the HARVEST BOOK, HOUGHTON MIFFLIN HARCOURT PUBLISHING COMPANY, 215 Park Avenue South, New York, New York 10003).

Woolf's circular argumentation style is what makes this book unique. I have attempted to demonstrate this by constantly citing extracts from the volume. If these tend to weigh the text down, the original, in contrast is light and humorous, although it is not an easy read. After reading my initial remarks, those who are at least intending to read *Three Guineas* (which is certainly worth doing), could skip this chapter and move on to the more important third chapter, where I discuss Virginia Woolf's novels. They are certainly a pleasure to read and it is worth trying to read at least a few paragraphs in English to see for yourself how the language gets body in her writing.

Lario Sinigaglia

CHAPTER ONE

CARL GUSTAV JUNG'S TYPES

Psychological types

This is the title of a wide-ranging volume written by C.G. Jung.

Although it is a demanding read, I recommend this book as it provides an interpretative grid for the human mind, demonstrating the way in which certain key characteristics either tend to combine with other key characteristics or overshadow them.

It is precisely this affinity or incompatibility of innate characteristics that produces psychological types.

They are then developed or repressed by environmental factors.

In this book, I offer but a brief summary, one that cannot do justice to Jung's work of genius, which runs to hundreds of pages, and really needs to be read to be appreciated.

Jung begins by dividing individuals into "introverts" and "extroverts" (general types), this being the main distinction.

The extrovert's "libido" (attraction, direction and existential awareness) is focused on the outer object, while the introvert's "libido" is focused on the inner object. This does not only mean focusing on oneself.

According to Jung, human interiority is actually inhabited by archetypes, namely primordial images that although subconscious, constitute a population's collective heritage.

Even the extrovert, of course, shares the collective heritage of images, but the value of this imagery is sought externally. The introvert, on the other hand, does have some contact with the external, but attributes value to the object according to an internal process of deliberation.

Four key psychic functions are then assigned to, and made use of by, both introvert and extrovert types: sensation, intuition, thinking and feeling.

The first two are non-rational and the latter two are rational.

The distinction is as follows: the first two functions (sensation and intuition) supply the material that is developed by the other two (thinking and feeling).

If sensation is focused on the appreciation of perceived appearances, intuition is focused on secondary, larval appearances (yet to become apparent).

Intuition is based on certain established markers in the evolution of reality that can sometimes be discovered using small clues. It sheds light on the unknown, especially the future.

But the price is being almost blind to what is clearly visible. Tiresias, the blind prophet who features in many Greek plays, embodies this function nicely.

Thinking and feeling are both rational functions.

It could be said that objectives are identified by thinking whilst values are identified by feeling.

That thinking requires a certain detachment, whilst feeling requires involvement and closeness.

That the former allows for complex strategies leading to the acquisition of a resource, whilst the latter is always focused on defending a value.

I have now identified eight key types according to the dominant general type, introversion or extroversion, and the main instrument used: intuition, sensation, thinking or feeling.

Individuals are nevertheless more complex, in the sense that they must use at least one irrational capability, and simultaneously, one non-rational capability in order to function on an existential level.

Indeed, what would Tiresias do were he unable to develop his intuitions (essentially visions) intellectually in order to give voice to them in the form of prophecies?

Could the feeling of a mother towards her children be explained if her senses had never registered their existence?

How would politicians defend the institutions that their feeling tells them are important if their intuition did not determine the threats facing such institutions?

Since each key function can be paired with either of the two complementary functions (only one of the two rational functions can match up with a non-rational function and vice versa), there will consequently be sixteen distinct key psychological types.

I must highlight the fact that the psychic functions (sensation, intuition, thinking and feeling) are not dominant or secondary in themselves, but only in relation to the individual who makes use of them.

If we then take cultural influences into account (which develop or repress innate dispositions), the fact that the quantity of innate functions is unpredictable and, finally, the fact that a complementary rejected function still has a secondary function that becomes relevant when the adopted psychic model is in crisis (in other words, in extremely important moments), then step-by-step we can gain a better understanding of how complex reality is. And also how fundamentally indescribable it is.

("Psychological types" is a passage from the fifth chapter of *La Falce di Crono* by Lario Sinigaglia, Armando Editore, Rome 2009)

This is how Jung portrays the human psychological types.

I should specify that Jung's portrayal assumes a state of consciousness: this means that if a function is said to be *prevalent* in an individual, it is by implication the function that the individual most often applies consciously. But the recessive functions do not disappear. They are absorbed, so to say, by the subconscious, where they operate nonetheless. And whether they operate *well* or *badly* depends on the space the conscious mind makes available for its own subconscious. In short: when you play the game we call life, you must make choices. It is, however, also necessary to respect the choices *that were not made* to avoid becoming dangerously unilateral. The ancient Greeks called this excess *Hybris* and believed it would immediately be punished.

(Whether or not you believe in the Gods, excess will without fail be punished by circumstances)

You must therefore leave space for your own subconscious.

Thus far, I have only outlined what Jung himself wrote in much more eloquent fashion. We will now try to make our own way along one of the avenues opened up by Jung.

The types are a family portrait that, like any other, exhibits a chronology and conceals a hierarchy.

The chronology.

Can it be said that some *types* are more ancient than others? In a certain sense, it can. As long as you understand that the chronological time shown on clocks, traced by history and allocated to periods that pre-date mankind, is a relatively recent conventiona way of seeing things that should in turn be contemplated and not blindly accepted.

We consider the first historian to be Herodotus (Greek, fifth century B.C.). There were certainly others before him both from inside and outside the area that we call the *West,* whose work has not been preserved. What is certain, though, is that historians have been around as long as history i.e. not very long.

Before that time, existence was not the continuous unravelling of a thread. It came wrapped up in its own cycles: suns, moons, seasons, generations, a notion perfectly captured in myth.

A chronology of types would certainly take place in a mythical time, that which saw the male separated from the female, as Greek mythology demonstrates with unparalleled drama.

I discussed this in the book *La falce di Crono* (Armando Editore, Roma, 2009; ebook Youcanprint Editore, Tricase (LE) 2015).

I must make this clear though: the *male* that is separate from the *female* is a psyche that defines itself in relation to another. I propose that there is a female psyche, which was and is dominant, and a separate male psyche that was and is secondary. These psyches are not linked to a person's physical sex, even though there is a reason for naming them according to sex, which will be demonstrated later on.

The female psyche is *dominant* not only in a chronological sense, but also in a *hierarchical* sense, the latter being the more important given that it is true of the present day and not just prehistoric times.

I must furthermore specify that the female psyche enjoys a *de facto* dominance, as you will see, even though society attributes more importance to the male psyche in reality, if not by law.

But let us now address what truly counts: hierarchy.

The hierarchy

Jung limits himself to stating that types of *feeling* are mainly female and types of *thinking* are for the most part male.

You will recall that the *feeling* and *thinking* functions are said to be *rational* as they develop, each in their own way, the material obtained by the perceptive – and therefore *non-rational* – functions. You will also recall that the two forms of rationality are incompatible *in the same individual*.

But being *individually incompatible* does not by any means imply that they are *socially incompatible*.

Indeed, human sociability expresses itself above all in the fact that individuals with different gifts benefit from interactions with spouses, friends and colleagues.

You might believe that in relationships between a *rational* type and a *non-rational* type, the former is usually *the leader* since he or she has a natural tendency to organise.

But, of all of the pairings, one is particularly important because of its functional and cognitive effectiveness: the pairing of two rational types, for example a *feeling* female and a *thinking* male.

In order to understand the way in which the couple will probably collaborate, it is necessary to reflect on the way in which *feeling* and *thinking* interact.

Feeling

I previously said that feeling identifies values and therefore simultaneously identifies non-values. But the quality of having values/non-values is different from the many others possessed by individuals. Rather, for the *feeling person*, it is the prerequisite for the very existence of the individuals.

It is in fact clear that none of us perceives everything that is possible, but we reliev only that which, positively or negatively, is important and moment by moment automatically disregarded that is irrelevant.

So if I substitute the impersonal words *value/non-value* with the more engaging words *love/hate* (there are obviously grey areas), you will understand that love and hate are the architects of an individual *cosmogony*: they create the world we live in.

Furthermore, love tends to retain its own object.

From a theological point of view, love is the main creator, as well as the main custodian of everything that exists, since it is the result of the feeling that stems from individuals and their union.

On the other hand, *to love* is to take part in something and therefore identify one or more other parts that in turn contribute to a general balance, along with your own feelings, that is made up of imbalances. To put it more simply: they contribute to the foundation and preservation of *being* as it actually is.

But if *love* creates and preserves, what transforms or presumes to transform?

Thinking

It is necessary to understand the nature of *thinking,* which according to the prevailing understanding is not one of the rational functions, but is rationality itself.

On the other hand, thinking can perform its function by projecting a network of equivalences onto the *being.*

I will start by examining the rational function of language, which is fundamental for thinking.

To simplify things as much as possible: language identifies entities , that is to say *individuals,* through what is said (i.e. what is predicated) using characteristics (adjectives) or actions (verbs). In general, what is attributed to individuals by language is termed the *predicate.*

To identify means: "finding the material or conceptual profile of the entity", so that the characteristic or action can be accurately attributed to the individual.

If we separate language from verbs and adverbs (which are a type of adjective associated with verbs), adjectives, prepositions and conjunctions (which clearly have a syntactic function, this being their role in the sentence), we are left with words that describe individuals.

Individuals are the very subjects of rational language.

We sometimes attribute a *proper noun* to individuals (by law), places (for convenience), certain animals (for sentimental reasons) and even some objects. Beyond the relatively limited linguistic category of *proper nouns,* there is the extensive *common noun* category. Beyond the linguistic category of *common nouns,* there is the unimaginably vast linguistic category of *nameless* individuals.

But is the latter a linguistic category? Certainly, since language has the means to express the concept and certainly does so when necessary i.e. when human feeling embellishes that which has no name and brings it into linguistic existence. But that is *existence* itself.

Let us linger on the subject of *common nouns.*

Through the *common noun,* language brings together a set of individuals who are assumed to have some sort of *similarity,* despite each individual being distinguishable from others.

This similarity is extremely important for forming rational language i.e. language that is logical and based on rational thought.

Sets of individuals and *sets of sets* are the objects of the oft-mentioned, but relatively unknown *set theory,* which is commonly believed to be the very foundation of rationality.

Common nouns and the *descriptions that feature common nouns* are used by language to define *sets* and are called *intensions,* whilst the *sets* themselves are called *extensions* (of the respective *intensions*).

But to return to good old everyday language, we are ultimately talking about *concepts* that describe *objects* and their *qualities* and the *actions* associated with them.

You will note that there is a huge gap between the *concepts* and *objects* that they relate to.

It is the same jump we make between the *Irises* painted by Van Gogh and those sold in bunches by florists.

The jump between the *water lilies* from Monet's Giverny garden, those that the artist captured just before the light in his eyes went out and those that fishermen push aside with their boats as they search for the best position from which to cast their lines.

And yet *irises* and *water lilies* are one and the same.

But Van Gogh's irises and Monet's water lilies exist (in a painting) because the artists loved and were in tune with natural flowers, driving them to create unique and sublime works of art that enable each of us to "see" irises and water lilies, perhaps for the first time.

These works of art are "non-calculable" because they come from inside and outside of the calculable world: it is more like the world described in Genesis: "And God saw everything that he had made, and behold it was very good" (Genesis 1, 31)

The fact that works of art also have a very high commercial value is almost a reflection of what we have been talking about: in fact, such works of art are usually neither sold nor bought, and if it does happen, the buyer is in reality purchasing the prestige associated with owning the piece.

A florist might love irises, but you do not need to love them to sell them in bunches. The basic requirements for making a profit are actually a minimal amount of economic planning and some calculations.

Fishermen might also love water lilies, but once again this is not necessary given that carps, who swim lazily between the long stems of water lilies, are what drives them to sail amongst the flowers.

Calculation

The characteristic rationality that is expressed through thinking is what we term *calculation*, and all types of judgement (be it logical, arithmetical or the application of set theory) require prior preparation of the materials to which they are to be applied. This preparation entails grouping objects into *concepts* for logical calculation or into *sets* for set theory and arithmetical calculation, meaning that they become homogenised. Here there is no space for the incalculability that is typical of feeling.

In fact, feeling *creates* without profit whilst thinking selects what it believes to be advantageous.

Feeling is constituent because the objects it creates form the subject's *existential awareness* and the special rationality that is characteristic of feeling is focused on caring and protecting.

Sacrifice is also contemplated by this rationality and consequently so is destruction, but *making a sacrifice* actually means *making* someone or something *sacred* simply in order to provide better protection.

On the other hand, the *aims* of thinking are optional insomuch as they are either achievable or unachievable depending on the opportunity cost calculation carried out by the individual: the more accurate the judgement is, the more detached from it the subject will be.

Therefore, not only are objects homogenised to make calculation possible, they usually do not even feature in the subject's emotional sphere, which acts as an agent for authentic or false values (the latter of which go against the subject's nature) or artificial values (which are not usually in the subject's nature).

Gain is an example of a false value whilst "ideology" is the concept under which fictitious values are classified.

Ideology actually provides collective fake values for those who have none and is the main means of manipulating people.

Female mind and male mind

I have gone through the *Psychological Types* and examined the functions defined by Jung as *rational* (feeling and thinking), which develop the content acquired by the *irrational* functions (sensory perception and intuition).

When it comes to single individuals, Jung's characterisation is of course evenly distributed, with each individual having a key function that defines their type and a secondary function that is compatible with the first.

Incompatibility can be defined as follows: the two *rational* functions cannot coexist in one individual because they are antithetical, as seen previously.

The incompatibility between the two *irrational* functions is similar.

But I now want to prepare a model of social interaction between the types that demonstrates the psychology of *social individuals.* These are unions between people that have their own functional individuality and sometimes receive social recognition: the *legal personality.*

Jung himself observes that one of the irrational functions, *intuition,* is not considered to be that important in modern times because facts take precedence and consequently so do the present moment and brief periods of time: if the prophets of Israel were revived today, they would not have an audience.

Sensory perception therefore takes precedence from a social perspective: intuitive people exist, but have little standing even within their own family.

But perhaps this is not a new fact: Apollo gave Cassandra the gift of foresight because he loved her, but then bestowed on her the torment of never being believed to because she rejected his advances.

Thus, from a social perspective, the two *rational* functions (feeling and thinking) mainly draw on sensory perception.

But, for the reasons stated above, the *rational* functions are not on the same hierarchical level.

Or rather: *they would not* be on the same level if *we lived* in a world based on feeling; but this situation occurs neither in total nor in part due to a *long-term* issue, which I will try to explain.

I will begin by stating that a mind whose main function is *feeling* is defined as a *female mind,* whilst a mind whose main function is *thinking* is defined as a *male mind.*

What link does such a classification have with concrete facts? In other words: with a person's physical sex?

We must observe that the physical sex of human beings, although it is the only type to be legally recognised, is not the best way to access the psychic dimension. It nevertheless seems that physical sex, a rough indicator, can be re-classified as follows:

- The *feeling* psychological type is often seen in individuals of the female sex where it is usually of a high quality.

- The *thinking* psychological type is often seen in individuals of the male sex, but is not usually of a high quality. In fact, few individuals of either the male or female sex are high quality thinking types.

The functional problem of *thinking* is the connection with *feeling,* which is the true determining function. But this is in essence the problem of the missing connection between the *male psyche* and the *female psyche.*

In conclusion: I define the *female psyche* as the one in which the *feeling* function prevails because as a creative function, it is hierarchically prevalent. In effect, *feeling creates* the reality that only later *is judged through thinking.*

In recent years (that is to say from historical times onwards), *thinking* has gained legitimacy and even social prevalence. At the same time there has been an increase in the social importance of individuals for whom *thinking* is a key rational function. I will now briefly expand upon how this has come about:

1) From the beginning, the male social role was inferior to the female social role, as demonstrated in Greek myth through the Dactyls: these are males who protect and aid the Mother Goddess whilst she creates the gods. This is presented in myth as a physical subordination, but in reality it is a psychic subordination since it is the female psyche that identifies the fundamental values and the male psyche that is servile.

2) In recent times (around the beginning of recorded history), societies became much more complex and allowed for the development of thinking strategies as well as the availability of time as a resource, typically by male individuals. Males, of course, do not have reproductive duties, or rather their role is carried out quickly, even when it comes to educating their children.

3) In social terms, thinking is a complementary faculty (this contrasts with the individual, for whom it can be a dominant faculty): males are dedicated to *thinking* just as females are dedicated to *feeling,* and thinking is one of the ways in which a male may serve females. But, from a certain point in his life, he also serves society, religion, the company he works for and many other dubious institutions.

4) Thinking also serves thinking itself in a typical case of the servant creating a bad master. All things considered, philosophy would still be a harmless activity had it not become involved with science and technology, whose ambiguous contributions can no longer be restricted.

Over the course of this process the link between *feeling* and *thinking* is either relaxed or broken, with the latter assuming a type of autonomy that is demonstrated in the fact that it pushes *gain* or *ideology* to the forefront of its own existential development.

They are not one and the same since *gain* is not an ideology, but instead bestows the dignity of an *objective* on a *method.*

Ideology, on the other hand, is a fictitious value that is instilled precisely because it is identified through thinking rather than feeling.

In the 20th Century, technology has afforded ideologies the means to carry out unprecedented massacres.

CHAPTER TWO

THREE GUINEAS BY VIRGINIA WOOLF

I believe that Virginia explains with particular sincerity both the female nature and the nature of the English language. For this reason, I would like to talk about her from more of a philosophical and psychological perspective than a literary one.

It is, of course, the high literary quality of her novels, or at least some of her novels, that lends them to a variety of interpretations.

Three Guineas

The work is complex, in contrast to the straightforward decisions about the people to whom the three guineas worth of donations should be sent. This is the sum that a benefactor (Virginia herself) contemplates donating towards efforts to avert the outbreak of a war — or rather the War — which looked likely to become as global and devastating as the Great War, as the First World War, which ended in 1918, was known. Virginia wrote during the period 1937-1938. As is common knowledge, the war broke out a short time later — Germany invaded Poland in 1939 and the French and British allies consequently declared war on Germany — and was far more bloody and destructive than the Great War. Moreover, it signalled a violent end to human co-habitation and brought the demonic aspects of technology to light. Virginia did not see the end of the war because on 28 March 1941, she drowned herself in the familiar waters of the River Ouse, which flowed past her home in Rodmell, Southern England. Virginia suffered bouts of depression and was certainly unsettled by the forays of the German bombers that, during the course of the Battle of Britain (1940), flew over her home in Rodmell, Sussex and destroyed her house in London.

It is worth analysing the book from different perspectives, ordered by increasing importance:

a)   The conclusions and established conditions;
b)   The reasons for the conclusions;
c)   The arguments;
d)   The style;
e)   The omissions;

Virginia uses a rhetorical device to develop her arguments that may well be based on real events.

She responds to a letter from a solicitor, the chair of a cultural society aiming to develop initiatives in order to prevent the outbreak of war, a war that did indeed then come to pass in the form of the "Second World War". The solicitor suggests three alternative ways in which Virginia could support the society: endorsing a public appeal promoting the society (Virginia is famous and her endorsement is therefore of particular value), registering as a member of the society and providing financial support.

She replies to these proposals by writing a text entitled *Three Guineas,* which runs to around two hundred pages, and sending three guineas — or rather three cheques to the value of one guinea each and an accompanying letter — to three societies. Virginia spent around three years writing the text alongside other projects.

Only the third cheque is sent to the solicitor's society. The first two are sent to two society treasurers, who had also written to Virginia to request financial support for their projects: the renovation of a women's university college and a truly modest request for Virginia to pay the rent for the headquarters of a society that supports women who wish to find work and, consequently, make money in the liberal professions.

But what counts is that each of the three guineas, apparently used to support different initiatives, are actually used to support the solicitor's initiative, or rather to oppose the imminent war. The way in which these heterogeneous acts come together to serve a common goal is the main thrust of Virginia's argument.

It is widely acknowledged that every argument veers towards an outcome, or rather its own conclusion. In the case of *Three Guineas,* however, neither the recipients of the sums of money nor even the complex reasons have any significant bearing. What has a truly great bearing is the way in which the reasons are written as this makes *Three Guineas* a cleverly disguised work of art on the one hand, and an equally well-disguised exercise in philosophy on the other. But what is the device that apparently both conceals and reveals the masterpiece?

It is "a text that is full of deviations, interludes, hiatuses and a style of reasoning whereby the thread is continuously lost, yet never truly lost, this being the book's other unique feature" (from the introduction to *Le tre ghinee* by Luisa Muraro, Feltrinelli 1992).

The book's first unique feature is, of course, the fact that Virginia barely alludes to the causes that were and are still considered to be responsible for the outbreak of the conflict: fascism and militarism.

It is therefore a challenging book that presents an original point of view and a wealth of opinions by means of an apparently disjointed and inefficient argument. This is a book that should consequently be read and re-read.

First of all, what is a guinea?

It was the highest-value coin produced by the United Kingdom's Royal Mint. Today it has no legal value, but certainly has an economic value given that it was a gold coin weighing around 8 grams. We can visualise this by thinking of the well-known gold pound coins (known as *sovereigns*), which weigh more or less the same. The market value of a gold pound coin is approximately 270 euros, but they obviously have a sentimental value, which is why many people collect them. The guinea has an even greater sentimental value: certain important sentimental assets such as racehorses or paintings, which are fought over in authorised auction houses, are in fact listed in guineas. In short, the very word 'guinea' has an *important sentimental* value that is not adequately demonstrated by its market value.

Guineas are rare; guineas are valuable — Virginia repeats — which is why when sending the guineas, she imposes conditions on the recipients. Yet these conditions do not apply to all, only to the female treasurers of the female societies: none are imposed on the solicitor, as we will see.

But it is first of all necessary to examine her reasons for making the donations.

Virginia takes a truly broad approach. Since she wants, and is obliged, to write a letter in response to that sent by the solicitor, she begins by creating an image of her interlocutor, who has been waiting three years for the reply: this is the time that it took Virginia to write *Three Guineas,* which is the reply.

Virginia knows that every dialogue must have a common basis from which an understanding can be reached and that using the same language, the English language in this case, is not sufficient as a common basis if the interlocutors do not share common experience. *Understanding*, here, is not meant in the sense of forming an agreement of some sort, rather merely grasping the meaning of other people's words. Comprehension is a necessary precursor to every possible agreement.

Virginia begins by listing the existing common bases, which are many and profound: we both come from the educated classes, we speak with the same accent, we use a knife and fork in the same manner, we talk about the same things at the table, we have similar relationships with the servants and therefore ...

we could marry one another without raising eyebrows, this seems to imply.

Virginia continues: we both live from the fruits of our professional activities, but although this fact is crucial for creating a basis of understanding: *"But … those three dots mark a precipice, a gulf so deeply cut between us that for three years and more I have been sitting on my side of it wondering whether it is any use to try to speak across it"* (Three Guineas, 1966, - a HARVEST BOOK, HOUGHTON MIFFLIN HARCOURT PUBLISHING COMPANY, 215 Park Avenue South, New York, New York 10003 - page 4)

When she then comes to clarify the nature of the abyss, she invites Mary Kingsley to speak: *"I don't know if I ever revealed to you the fact that being allowed to learn German was all the paid-for education I ever had. Two thousand pounds was spent on my brother's, I still hope not in vain."* (ibid.)

But who is Mary Kingsley? Virginia explains in a note, the first in a series of lengthy, extremely well-researched notes: she was an 19th century English writer from an educated, affluent family. Negligible sums were spent on her education, but like Virginia, she could rely on her father's well-stocked library. The note informs us of other similar cases.

But immediately afterwards Virginia informs us about the existence of *Arthur* and *Arthur's Education Fund.* Naturally — Virginia observes — the solicitor has read *Pendennis,* a novel by William Thackeray (1811-1863, author of the better-known novel *Vanity* Fair) about Arthur and the fund of the same name. But since the reader of *Three Guineas* has probably not read *Pendennis,* unlike the solicitor, Virginia explains that it is about a fund, that is to say savings that every English family has been accumulating since the thirteenth century to pay for Arthur's studies. Arthur is the son, the imaginary firstborn, but there may be other sons who are guaranteed similar rights. However, in truth, Arthur is not only entitled to his studies, but also to a complete education that allows him to successfully integrate into a conservative and classist society. Arthur therefore must practise sport, expand his cultural knowledge and open his mind through travel, make favourable acquaintances in order to integrate professionally and politically and be provided with an allowance to allow him to live away from home: the family deals with all of these costly activities by means of *Arthur's Education Fund*.

Given that this does not concern and is not the entitlement of Arthur's sister although she was born into the same family — and is born into every family *of the same class,* she who suffers from the frugality that is required to provide resources to Arthur and whose only hope is a good marriage, assuming she does not have to tend to elderly parents or other relations in need of care — her impression of things is entirely different to Arthur's.

It is not possible to follow Virginia in her digressions, her interludes and her often humorous, but never sarcastic or resentful notes: *Three Guineas* really must be read and re-read.

Indeed, the goal of this book is not to summarise the content of *Three Guineas,* but to form a picture of the philosophical perspective, or rather the *general* perspective, even though Virginia's arguments are always, and not by chance, *specific*.

Furthermore, Virginia is always constructive and therefore, although she doubts that she can reach an understanding with the solicitor, she throws a gangway across the abyss that separates them, that separates Arthur from his sister, by sending him a letter (i.e. *Three Guineas*) and one of the guineas, but without imposing any conditions upon him, save one, which is implied: read *Three Guineas* **and translate it** since the letter is not written in the language that the solicitor would have used had he wanted to communicate the message, even though it is written in English, the language spoken by both interlocutors, who are part of the same educated class.

This is, in my opinion, the book's most profound meaning: it shows that the English language needs to be translated within itself i.e. from English into English. But only Arthur's English exists, not that spoken by his sister, so Virginia gives form to the English language used by Arthur's sister by writing *Three Guineas.*

In truth, she did not only do this in *Three Guineas,* but also, and more extensively, in other literary works. However, the recipients of the other books are unknown, as if they were letters sealed in a bottle and entrusted to the sea's waves. This book, on the other hand, does have a recipient, the solicitor, Arthur himself, whose sister has already given much over the centuries and today is sending him a guinea and a letter written in an unknown language: the English language.

The first thing to explain to the solicitor is why two whole guineas, the first two, were sent to two treasurers of societies that carry out activities in aid of women, rather than him. In itself, this should not concern the solicitor, given that the precious guineas belong to Virginia. But Virginia wants the solicitor to understand that even the first two guineas have an objective that coincides with that of the third: the solicitor did not understand this then and does not understand it today because he did not translate the accompanying letter. It is not even certain that the treasurers of those societies fully understand Virginia's intentions and she does in fact impose conditions on the recipients; such conditions, if they are acknowledged, will give these recipients rightful ownership of the guineas, beyond their physical possession of them. If those conditions are not acknowledged, they might as well buy rags and petrol with the guineas and burn the material forms of their initiatives (which are buildings) given that the results would in any case be disastrous.

The first guinea

Virginia's reasoning does not follow a linear trajectory starting with a premise and ending with a conclusion, but follows the strange circular movement of certain breezes that destroy nothing but touch, shake and move everything.

There are no premises, only the opinions of Virginia or qualified witnesses who share their views with us. Even when some of these opinions are not shared by Virginia, they are recounted with the respect that each deserves and are at least used to demonstrate that these positions are incompatible.

This incompatibility it not discussed, but is instead expressed through a sense of wonder and unfamiliarity: *"Your world, then, the world of professional, of public life, seen from this angle undoubtedly looks queer."* (ibid., 18)

At first glance this world is extremely impressive as crowded together in a small area are St Paul's Cathedral, the Bank of England, City Hall, the ramparts of the Royal Courts of Justice and a little distance away, Westminster Abbey and the Houses of Parliament.

Standing on *London Bridge* and contemplating the scene, Virginia — or one of the daughters or sisters of educated men — is thinking that her own father and brothers have been climbing those steps for hundreds of years, entering and exiting through those doors to hold debates, administer justice and make money and that her own house owes its creed, laws, clothing, carpets and roast dinners to those institutions.

But, entering on tip-toe, the first impression of those colossal dimensions and that majestic architecture shatters into a thousand moments of wonder at the ceremonies that take place there and the gowns that are worn.

Once again: it is wrong and futile to summarise Virginia's arguments when she is navigating the symbolic ceremonial rituals and the bizarre and incomprehensible selection of official male attire and pointing out that it has a different function from that of women's robes, whose primary function is to elicit male admiration. This makes it impossible to understate the importance of these robes given that they enable her to embark on the only career permitted to a woman: marriage.

The function of male attire is instead to promote, so to say, what it contains, like *the tickets in a grocer's shop*: its function is hence to advertise. If women use their clothing in this manner, it is judged unbecoming and improper.

And it is not by chance that the most ostentatious uniforms, which are consequently more attractive to young men, are the uniforms that soldiers wear. This is another demonstration of the strange male attraction to war.

Enormous sums of money are invested in male cultural institutions (the prestigious and expensive private schools of Eton, Harrow, Winchester and Rugby and the famous universities of Oxford and Cambridge). Yet these sums are no match for the even greater amounts spent on military equipment. Is it therefore unjustified to make a connection between that culture and this militarism?

But what sense is there, Virginia wonders, in sending a sum of money to a treasurer who wishes to renovate a women's *college* if this is what culture leads to? Would it not be preferable to invest the money in matches and petrol with which to set fire to the college?

This is what Virginia begins to write in the letter addressed to the treasurer, but what she sends to the treasurer is not written in those terms. She instead recounts this to the solicitor, because her letter to him is the most important. It is the solicitor to whom she must explain that the first two guineas, which were sent to the treasurers of the female institutions, will help, or at least might help, to prevent the imminent war. This is precisely what the solicitor would like, but involves a method that the solicitor has not requested and does not understand. For this reason, the letter sent to him is more complex. Or rather: even though the letter is written in English, it is so complex that a translation into English is required because it emanates from a different type of mind. This latter difference is unlike normal individual differences.

Virginia understands that in the women's *colleges*, it is not possible to teach a radically different culture to that taught at Eton and Harrow due to economic constraints, although that would be desirable. It is not realistic because women must first of all have the ability to keep themselves, and only when they enjoy economic independence and are no longer constrained to accept the opinions of their fathers, brothers and husbands for economic reasons, will they be able to express their own unique points of view.

Without being restricted to an indirect form of influence on worldly matters exercised by means of their own female charm, without being subjected to humiliating procedures such as inviting possible suitors to lunch.

"The influence of the pheasant upon love alone deserves a chapter to itself." (ibid., 38)

It would be better if, at the *colleges*, different teachers created a different culture focused on integration rather than specialisation, on human relationships rather than technology, a *college* without diplomas, without competition or vanity, but … it is not practical, only a nice idea, to impose a similar condition on the busy treasurer so that she can take possession of the guinea. She must therefore take it and do what she can.

Also because, after all, it is not necessary to teach women differently given that *"law and practice have developed that difference, whether innate or accidental."* (ibid., 6)

The difference will thus emerge of its own accord when they are no longer economically conditioned.

How can the war be prevented? *"The answer based upon our experience and our psychology — Why fight? — is not an answer of any value. Obviously there is for you some glory, some necessity, some satisfaction in fighting which we have never felt or enjoyed."* (ibid.)

Incidentally: Virginia speaks to specific interlocutors about real experiences. In this case, she, the daughter of an educated man, addresses an educated man (the solicitor) and rather than proposing general solutions that will be universally applicable until the end of time (that is to say *ideological* solutions), she suggests a concrete type of behaviour that is fully reasoned. Can the daughters of nobles or working class men or farmers share Virginia's point of view? Perhaps.

The second guinea

*"Failing money", she goes on, "any gift will be acceptable —
books, fruit or cast-off clothing that can be sold in a bazaar."*
(ibid., 41)

Thus ends the letter from the honorary female treasurer of a
society that helps the daughters of educated men to find work
in the liberal professions.

Virginia's arguments are like a wave train, in which each
argument overlaps with the previous one and the final one
sends the guinea to the correct recipient. But, once again, all of
this is explained to the solicitor, to the educated brother of the
educated woman who sees things in her own way and speaks
another language. She therefore begins to write a second
letter to the female treasurer, which is simultaneously part of
the letter to the solicitor, to whom she needs to explain why
two whole guineas are not being sent to him, although they
are in fact being spent to help him achieve his objectives.

Virginia wonders why the letter is written in such a humble
tone, which is suggestive of poverty, unless the poverty is fake
and therefore a lie. It is in fact strange that the society is so
lacking in means given that women have had access to the
liberal professions, notoriously lucrative activities, for twenty
years (since 1919).

Indeed, the *Great War* that ended in 1918 saw millions of men
carted off to the front, opening the doors of civil society to
women: it was once again true that *every cloud has a silver
lining.*

But these are the concrete facts:

1) The W.S.P.U. (Women's Social Political Union: the most famous of the societies that won the right for women to vote from 1919 onwards) recorded its greatest ever income of 42,000 pounds in 1912.
2) A highly qualified female professional was unlikely to earn an annual salary of more than 250 pounds (in *A Room of One's Own* Virginia states her opinion that for an acceptable level of economic independence, an annual salary of at least 500 pounds is required).

The first figure must be compared to the far greater incomes of the Conservative Party and the Liberal Party. Even the Labour Party, to which the brothers of working-class women belong, has a substantially greater income than the W.S.P.U.

The second fact must be considered in the light of the salaries of liberal professionals and qualified public service employees, which always have at least three zeros.

The first fact suggests that little money is available to women.

The second fact suggests that educated working women are poorly paid. Perhaps because they only deserve a small salary?

Virginia calls two witnesses with conflicting opinions: the respected and detailed Whitaker's Almanack, which contains a list of civil servants and their salaries, and the Prime Minister, Mr Stanley Baldwin.

The Almanack, which contains information relating to salary payments, implies that women are third-rate civil servants, while the Prime Minister affirms that they are first-rate civil servants; and yet both are well-informed.

"Those to whose names the word 'Miss' is attached do not seem to enter the four-figure zone. The sex distinction seems, according to Whitaker, possessed of a curious leaden quality, liable to keep any name to which it is fastened circling in the lower spheres." (ibid., 48)

"'Miss' may carry with it the swish of petticoats, the savour of scent or other odour perceptible to the nose on the further side of the partition and obnoxious to it. What charms and consoles in the private house may distract and exacerbate in the public office. The Archbishops' Commission assures us that this is so in the pulpit. Whitehall [this is the road in London where the government's departments are located] *may be equally susceptible."* (ibid., 50)

The substance of the social contribution made by women is greatly appreciated — especially as it involves more than just labour — as long as it is carried out in the home and under male supervision.

But women are only paid for work undertaken outside of the home and it is surprising how the family's income is spent (remember that we are talking about significant earnings made from the work of educated men like the solicitor): donations to and membership costs for political parties, various sports, hunting grounds, cricket, football and clubs.

There are two possibilities: she is either the most altruistic being in the world since she spends her money on clubs and *colleges* from which she is excluded, sports that she does not practise, wines that she does not drink and cigars that she does not smoke or *"her spiritual right to a share of half of her husband's income peters out in practice to an actual right to board, lodging, and a small annual allowance for pocket money and dress."* (ibid., 56)

This is the reason for which the women's societies are so poor and is why the female treasurer deserves her guinea, but only if she accepts a moral duty.

There exists, in fact, a parasite, an insect or a worm which subverts civil cooperation: *"There we have in embryo the creature, Dictator as we call him when he is Italian or German, who believes that he has the right, whether given by God, Nature, sex or race is immaterial, to dictate to other human beings how they shall live; what they shall do."* (ibid., 53)

"And is not the woman who has to breathe that poison and to fight that insect, secretly and without arms, in her office, fighting the Fascist or the Nazi as surely as those who fight him with arms in the limelight of publicity? And must not that fight wear down her strength and exhaust her spirit? Should we not help her to crush him in our own country before we ask her to help us to crush him abroad?" (ibid.)

The moral duty is as follows: *"Think we must [...] Let us never cease from thinking — what is this 'civilisation' in which we find ourselves? What are these ceremonies and why should we take part in them? What are these professions and why should we make money out of them? Where in short is it leading us, the procession of the sons of educated men?"* (ibid., 62-63)

Virginia observes: *"And the facts disclosed above are of a kind to make us ask, before we write our cheque, whether if we encourage the daughters of educated men to enter the professions we shall not be encouraging the very qualities that we wish to prevent?"* (ibid., 58)

And again:

"We are here to consider facts. And the facts which we have just extracted from biography seem to prove that the professions have a certain undeniable effect upon the professors. They make the people who practise them possessive, jealous of any infringement of their rights, and highly combative if anyone dares dispute them." (ibid., 66)

And this is the first condition imposed on the beneficiary of the guinea:

"You shall swear that you will do all in your power to insist that any woman who enters any profession shall in no way hinder any other human being, whether man or woman, white or black, provided that he or she is qualified to enter that profession, from entering it; but shall do all in her power to help them." (ibid.)

But that is not all.

"You make money in them; that is true; but how far is money in view of those facts in itself a desirable possession? A great authority upon human life, you will remember, held over two

thousand years ago that great possessions were undesirable."
(ibid., 68)

Virginia examines the biographies of successful men and finds that:

"since 1914 I have never seen the pageant of the blossom from the first damson to the last apple — never once have I seen that in Worcestershire since 1914, and if that is not a sacrifice I do not know what is..." (ibid., 70)

It seems that the choice is between Scylla and Charybdis:

"Behind us lies the patriarchal system; the private house, with nullity, its immorality, its hypocrisy, its servility. Before us lies the public world, the professional system, with its possessiveness, its jealousy, its pugnacity, its greed." (ibid., 74)

Yet, in examining the biographies of a few women, she sees that there is a passage between the ruins of these opposing edifices because one resource has not been taken into account: even though savings were made on the education of these women, they received an education that came at no cost.

"And those teachers, biography indicates, obliquely, and indirectly, but emphatically and indisputably none the less, were poverty, chastity, derision, and — what word however covers 'lack of rights and privileges'? Shall we press the old word 'freedom' once more into service? 'Freedom from unreal loyalties then, was the fourth of their teachers; that freedom from loyalty to old schools, old colleges, old churches, old ceremonies, old countries which all those women enjoyed, and

which, to a great extent, we still enjoy by the law and custom of England. We have no time to coin new words, greatly though the language is in need of them. Let 'freedom from unreal loyalties' then stand as the fourth great teacher of the daughters of educated men." (ibid., 78)

These are thus the five conditions that the female treasurer must fulfil if she is to receive the guinea: that she help every person in possession of the necessary qualifications (not only women) to find professional work and that, in the practice of her profession, she refuse to surrender poverty, chastity, the derision of others and freedom from unreal loyalties.

"By poverty is meant enough money to live upon. That is, you must earn enough to be independent of any other human being and to buy that modicum of health, leisure, knowledge and so on that is needed for the full development of body and mind. But no more. Not a penny more.

By chastity is meant that when you have made enough money to live on by your profession you must refuse to sell your brain for the sake of money. That is you must cease to practise your profession, or practise it for the sake of research and experiment; or, if you are an artist, for the sake of the art; or give the knowledge acquired professionally to those who need it for nothing. But directly the mulberry tree begins to make you circle, break off. Pelt the tree with laughter.

By derision — a bad word, but once again the English language is much in need of new words — is meant that you must refuse all methods of advertising merit, and hold that ridicule, obscurity, and censure are preferable, for psychological reasons, to fame and praise. Directly badges, orders, or degrees are offered you, fling them back in the giver's face.

By freedom from unreal loyalties is meant that you must rid yourself of pride of nationality in the first place; also of religious pride, college pride, school pride, family pride, sex pride, and those unreal loyalties that spring from them. Directly the seducers come with their seductions to bribe you into captivity, tear up the parchments; refuse to fill up the forms. (ibid., 80)

We have reached the conclusion and Virginia makes the female treasurer aware that although many conditions seem to be attached to receiving the guinea, in reality there are only two: help every deserving and competent professional and refrain from earning excessive amounts given that English laws and customs will continue to provide the daughters of educated men with that tough and free education, which is sufficient to guarantee that the other conditions are respected.

We notice that Virginia turns disadvantage (tough education) into an advantage (the qualities that stem from it), but the reader may well be of the opinion that the conclusion becomes too optimistic, almost providential.

This is not the case: the current state of affairs can only be a good point of departure if it leads to a different type of awareness.

"As you know from your own experience, and there are facts that prove it, the daughters of educated men have always done

their thinking from hand to mouth; not under green lamps at study tables in the cloisters of secluded colleges. They have thought while they stirred the pot, while they rocked the cradle. It was thus that they won us the right to our brand new six-pence. It falls to us now to go on thinking; how are we to spend that sixpence? Think we must. Let us think in offices; in omnibuses; while we are standing in the crowd watching Coronations and Lord Mayor's Shows; let us think as we pass the Cenotaph; and in Whitehall; in the gallery of the House of Commons; in the Law Courts; let us think at baptisms and marriages and funerals. Let us never cease from thinking — what is this 'civilisation' in which we find ourselves? What are these ceremonies and why should we take part in them? What are these professions and why should we make money out of them? Where in short is it leading us, the procession of the sons of educated men?" (ibid., 62)

The third guinea

As you will remember, the solicitor had suggested three non-alternative possibilities to Virginia: endorse a public manifesto in which the signatories commit to "protecting culture and intellectual liberty"; become a member of the society; send a donation.

In reference to the invitation to endorse the society, Virginia maintains that in light of what has already been said, the request is absurd and that she is as amazed by it as Mary, the cook's hand in the Duke of Devonshire's kitchen, would be had the Duke, with his prestigious medals and his garter (an important decoration) told her: *"Stop your potato peeling, Mary, and help me to construe this rather difficult passage in Pindar."* (A Greek poet from the fifth century B.C., ibid).

But Mary's exclamation needs to be converted into the language of educated people; that is to say, once again, it is necessary to present a point of view to the solicitor that is unfamiliar to him. This point of view belongs to the sisters of the educated man, the well-known Arthur, to whose education, and therefore the cause of culture and intellectual liberty, they have contributed more than any other class of citizen, not only in England, but across Europe.

Now that a war is looming between the nations where the schools and universities at which Arthur studied (Eton, Harrow, Oxford, Cambridge, the Sorbonne, Heidelberg, Salamanca, Padua) are located *"ought you not, before you lease an office, hire a secretary, elect a committee and appeal for funds, to consider why those schools and universities have failed?*

That, however, is a question for you to answer. The question which concerns us is what possible help we can give you in protecting culture and intellectual liberty — we, who have been shut out from the universities so repeatedly, …., we who are, in fact, members not of the intelligentsia but of the ignorantsia?" (ibid., 87)

It is first of all necessary to explain what is meant by "culture" and "intellectual liberty".

(Virginia is now writing as though addressing one of the daughters of educated men, for all that she is technically addressing the solicitor).

"Therefore let us define culture for our purposes as the disinterested pursuit of reading and writing the English language. And intellectual liberty may be defined for our purposes as the right to say or write what you think in your own words, and in your own way." (ibid., 91)

An unrelated activity: *"But we would have you observe that the verb "to adulterate" means, according to the dictionary, "to falsify by admixture of baser ingredients." Money is not the only baser ingredient. Advertisement and publicity are also adulterers. Thus, culture mixed with personal charm, or culture mixed with advertisement and publicity, are also adulterated forms of culture. We must ask you to abjure them..."* (ibid., 94)

The right to say or write using our own words: *"we are in a lecture room, rank with the fumes of stale print, listening to a gentleman who is forced to lecture or to write every Wednesday, every Sunday, about Milton or about Keats, while the lilac shakes its branches in the garden free, and the gulls, swirling and swooping, suggest with wild laughter that such stale fish might with advantage be tossed to them."* (ibid., 99)

The war is looming (in 1936, the civil war had already begun in Spain, where the son of Virginia's sister, Vanessa Bell, would perish) and photos of corpses and ruined buildings appear daily: *"Can we bring out the connection between them and prostituted culture and intellectual slavery and make it so clear that the one implies the other, that the daughters of educated men will prefer to refuse money and fame, and to be the objects of scorn and ridicule rather than suffer themselves, or allow others to suffer, the penalties there made visible?"* (ibid., 95)

The daughters of educated men can use literature, the profession that is most accessible to them, to show that culture and intellectual liberty are contradictory to the war; but what might an ordinary female reader do?

"'[...] then you must adopt not active but passive methods of protecting culture and intellectual liberty.' 'And what may they be?' she will ask. 'To abstain, obviously. Not to subscribe to papers that encourage intellectual slavery; not to attend lectures that prostitute culture." (ibid., 98)

And not to endorse fanciful manifestos such as the one proposed by the solicitor, Virginia might have concluded, had the solicitor's education and her respect for him not held her back.

It is a mistake to join the society because there is a fundamental natural difference, sex, which is made greater by education.

"Different we are, as facts have proved, both in sex and in education. And it is from that difference, as we have already said, that our help can come, if help we can, to protect liberty, to prevent war. But if we sign this form which implies a promise to become active members of your society, it would seem that

we must lose that difference and therefore sacrifice that help."
(ibid., 103)

But it is not even right to set up another society.

"The very word 'society' sets tolling in memory the dismal bells of a harsh music: shall not, shall not, shall not. You shall not learn; you shall not earn; you shall not own; you shall not — such was the society relationship of brother to sister for many centuries... Inevitably we ask ourselves, is there not something in the conglomeration of people into societies that releases what is most selfish and violent, least rational and humane in the individuals themselves?... Inevitably we look upon societies as conspiracies that sink the private brother, whom many of us have reason to respect, and inflate in his stead a monstrous male, loud of voice, hard of fist..." (ibid., 105)

Unless it is a society of a radically different type.

"In the first place, this new society, you will be relieved to learn, would have no honorary treasurer, for it would need no funds. It would have no office, no committee, no secretary; it would call no meetings; it would hold no conferences. If name it must have, it could be called the Outsiders' Society. That is not a resonant name, but it has the advantage that it squares with facts — the facts of history, of law, of biography; even, it may be, with the still hidden facts of our still unknown psychology."
(ibid., 106)

The Outsiders' Society is distinguished by innate differences, by awareness, by choice. But, once again, the choices are also indicated, and paradoxically protected, by facts.

"As it is a fact that she cannot understand what instinct compels him, what glory, what interest, what manly satisfaction fighting provides for him... as fighting thus is a sex characteristic which she cannot share, the counterpart some claim of the maternal instinct which he cannot share, so is it an instinct which she cannot judge. The outsider therefore must leave him free to deal with this instinct by himself, because liberty of opinion must be respected, especially when it is based upon an instinct which is as foreign to her as centuries of tradition and education can make it." (ibid., 107)

Fight for one's own country? But *"how much of 'England' in fact belongs to her."* (ibid.)

"'For,' the outsider will say, 'As a woman my country is the whole world.' And if, when reason has said its say, still some obstinate emotion remains, some love of England dropped into a child's ears by the cawing of rooks in an elm tree, by the splash of waves on a beach, or by English voices murmuring nursery rhymes, this drop of pure, if irrational, emotion she will make serve her to give to England first what she desires of peace and freedom for the whole world." (ibid., 109)

"Broadly speaking, the main distinction between us who are outside society and you who are inside society must be that whereas you will make use of the means provided by your position — leagues, conferences, campaigns, great names, and all such public measures as your wealth and political influence place within your reach — we, remaining outside, will experiment not with public means in public but with private means in private." (ibid., 113)

"We have some reason to guide us in the guess that ease and freedom, the power to change and the power to grow, can only be preserved by obscurity; and that if we wish to help the human mind to create, and to prevent it from scoring the same rut repeatedly, we must do what we can to shroud it in darkness." (ibid., 114)

"Again, they will dispense with personal distinctions — medals, ribbons, badges, hoods, gowns — not from any dislike of personal adornment, but because of the obvious effect of such distinctions to constrict, to stereotype and to destroy. Here, as so often, the example of the Fascist States is at hand to instruct us — for if we have no example of what we wish to be, we have, what is perhaps equally valuable, a daily and illuminating example of what we do not wish to be." (ibid.)

But can the Outsiders' Society exist without buildings? Virginia thinks so and provides several examples taken from the press:

- Mrs Kathleen Rance, Mayor of Woolwich, declared in public: "I myself would not even do as much as darn a sock to help in a war".

- Miss E. R. Clarke, of the Board of Education, in a speech on the educational work carried out by large sporting associations, reminded the audience that female organizations for hockey, lacrosse, volleyball and cricket are subject to regulations which stipulate that the winning teams have no right to either trophies or prizes.

- Canon F.R. Barry, vicar of St. Mary the Virgin (the church at the University of Oxford) observed that in past centuries worshippers were predominantly female (75%), but that the situation is changing and young women are scarce in almost every Church of England congregation. Within the student population, young women are more distanced from the Church and the Christian faith than others of the same age.

"...considerable uneasiness at the attitude of educated men's daughters is apparent; and this experiment in passivity, whatever our belief in the value of the Church of England as a spiritual agency, is highly encouraging to us as outsiders. For it seems to show that to be passive is to be active; those also serve who remain outside. By making their absence felt their presence becomes desirable." (ibid., 119)

"Josephine Butler's label — Justice, Equality, Liberty — is a fine one; but it is only a label, and in our age of innumerable labels, of multi-coloured labels, we have become suspicious of labels; they kill and constrict. Nor does the old word 'freedom' serve, for it was not freedom in the sense of licence that they wanted; they wanted, like Antigone, not to break the laws, but to find the law Ignorant as we are of human motives and ill supplied with words, let us then admit that no one word expresses the force which in the nineteenth century opposed itself to the force of the fathers. All we can safely say about that force was that it was a force of tremendous power." (ibid., 138; J. Butler, English, was one of the suffragettes)

"To return then to the form that you have sent and ask us to fill up: for the reasons given we will leave it unsigned. But in order to prove as substantially as possible that our aims are the same as yours, here is the guinea, a free gift, given freely, without

any other conditions than you choose to impose upon yourself. It is the third of three guineas; but the three guineas, you will observe, though given to three different treasurers are all given to the same cause, for the causes are the same and inseparable." (ibid., 144)

These are the words that conclude and unify Virginia's digressions.

CHAPTER THREE

THE STRUCTURE OF VIRGINIA WOOLF'S NOVELS

Virginia's most innovative texts have these features:

1) Absence of a plot: in general, *nothing* happens; the *important* facts are omitted or downgraded (written in brackets).
2) There are no well-rounded descriptions of the characters, but their relationships, and therefore their link to the human and natural environment, are described. Characters are presented through the impressions they make and the feelings of other characters.
3) Places are described using metaphors, which are sometimes connected; the metaphorical link is presented as a character's point of view so that places and people mirror one another.
4) There is a temporal progression; present-day moments are recounted in the correct chronological order, but there are frequent and significant chronological gaps between each one. The past is presented as a memory, but the memory is related to a present-day feeling and is thus a present-day viewpoint.
5) Conversations have little relevance and are often partially omitted and replaced with ellipses. In the absence of words, important *unspoken* conversations, or communications, nevertheless take place between

interlocutors; not all of the communication that takes place is intentional. Much is communicated by accident, by actions and even by spoken words whose literal meaning is irrelevant.

6) There are preferred points of view that are more thoroughly and profoundly developed. In other words, there are main characters. But the numerous opinions expressed by secondary characters are important. Opinions and observations expressed by coincidental and almost random minor characters, who (paradoxically) appear to have nothing to do with the narrative, are frequently inserted, whilst at least one protagonist has no opinion whatsoever (Percival in *The Waves*).

7) Rational reflections are omitted: if they are spoken or thought by a protagonist, they are cited but not highlighted.

8) Feelings are not described, but are rather represented by metaphors or the physical effects they bring about.

This can be seen when just a handful of texts are examined:

JACOB'S ROOM, published in 1922: this was the first text in which Virginia gave form to a new sort of narration. It is about the short life of Jacob, who died on the front line in France during the First World War. Almost all that is left of him are the opinions of the people who knew him — some of whom were not close to him — and the clues from his empty rooms, which either say much or nothing to those who examine them. They are mainly about women, namely his mother. The nascent opinions of young Clara Durrant and Betty Flanders, the mother who is always too distant from her son, are very moving. It has been observed that Virginia reproduces the cubist painting style, which offers different viewpoints on the same object. It may be true if we acknowledge that only the viewpoints exist for Virginia, not the object. Jacob predates Percival, the protagonist of *The Waves* (published in 1931), the absent hero who only exists in his friends' memories.

MRS DALLOWAY, published in 1925: this text is about a single day during which Mrs D and her servants prepare for the party that will take place that evening and which draws to a close as the novel ends. A mysterious relationship develops — due to a certain amount of synchronicity — between Septimus Warren Smith, who will die in the afternoon, and Mrs D, who will survive for the time being. If I had to recommend just one book, this would be it.

TO THE LIGHTHOUSE, published in 1927: the narrative takes place over the course of ten years in a holiday home at the seaside where the Ramsay family and their friends stay on only the first and last day of the decade. On the first day, they plan a boat trip to the lighthouse island opposite the house and on the last day, they go on the trip. Ten years and the First World War have passed by in the meantime, taking the lives of some and leaving their mark on the others. Mrs Ramsay — the soul of the house and the prime mover of her guests — dies during the empty intermission, but is just as alive on the second day, when she is absent, as she was on the first, when she was present.

THE YEARS published in 1937: this is the story of the Pargiter family, photographed in eleven different moments separated by different time intervals over the course of fifty years. This is the time between the youth and old age of Eleanor Pargiter, who is at first the devoted and loving daughter of Colonel Abel (who loved her in return), but is then changed and set free by his death and her own nature, and inevitably becomes isolated. Eleanor is not the protagonist of the story, only the common thread that unites a family of lonely individuals, who are mysterious and naturally sterile, at least as far as children are concerned.

BETWEEN THE ACTS published in 1941: this is another text with a time span of one day, the day prior to a stage performance that involves the local community and takes place in the grand old house of Bartholomew Oliver, a former officer in the Indian Army (as was Colonel Pargiter). In the time leading up to the play and during the intervals, the different points of view of the owners of the house and their guests unfold before us. The play is staged using modest means, but in line with the ambitious aims of the author and director Miss La Trobe, a lonely and particularly pensive woman. Her message, however, barely interrupts the audience's customary lethargy. This is Virginia's farewell as she did not live to see the book published.

*****

Whilst these books are intended for a sophisticated audience, they have been widely appreciated for a long time: Virginia Woolf is unanimously considered to be a pioneer of the literary genre.

It is not my intention to reproduce, on this subject, what others have already said much better than I ever could. I will instead bring together the philosophical and psychological meaning of Virginia's artistic revolution.

She is a writer, so she uses language as a means of expression; she is a writer of fiction and her goal is therefore to convey reality rather than her own subjectivity or even the aesthetical possibilities of language, as we would expect of a poet.

Virginia wants to reveal reality to us, or at least an aspect of reality that has not hitherto been conveyed. Upon finishing one of her novels, this seems to be precisely what we have gained, along with an aesthetic enjoyment of her work.

What does the reality revealed by Virginia therefore consist of?

It has at least two aspects: one philosophical and one psychological.

The philosophical aspect

Virginia uses language in an original way in that she uses it in a way that is unnatural in any language.

We can observe, incidentally, that thinking and acting *unnaturally* is a typically human characteristic.

But Virginia uses language in an unnatural way to show women, and especially men, a means of expression that is different to rationality, a foreign language that is perhaps suited to *Outsiders.*

But for the time being, let us pause to consider language.

Every language has its own conceptual nature and a narrative function. We will see below, given that it is one of the conclusions of this book, that not all languages are equal, although it is true that their main function is to *recount* something to someone by referring to *concepts.*

There is nothing unusual about concepts: every word is a concept, with the exception of conjunctions and prepositions.

On the contrary, we must reconsider every word as a concept that has crystallised into language through common usage. There is, furthermore, an infinite number of other concepts, the expression of which requires a plurality of words. If changes in circumstance bring such concepts into common use, however, we can expect that new words will be coined to express them more concisely.

An increase or reduction in the number of words (some concepts also become redundant), is commonplace since words are proposed and accepted: use implies acceptance.

Other than common words that are exchanged across the entire linguistic area, there are words known as *proper nouns* that are exchanged in naturally more limited linguistic areas to specifically refer to a person, entity or thing. This does not, however, apply to all words that are referred to by the same *common nouns.*

We should not worry about *proper nouns*: even these, like common nouns, are concepts, although their *meaning is limited.*

<u>We should thus use the term *concept,* always remembering that we are talking about well-known, informal words that are in daily use.</u>

A concept is therefore a label and a representation of a category of individuals (dogs, balls, children...), actions (verbs) or properties (adjectives) used in speech; these categories are well-known, but only in a general sense, by those who live in the same linguistic area.

Anyone who speaks has faith that the listeners are familiar with the word used (the concept!) and that they associate a real experience with it: in other words, that they know its meaning.

The speaker uses common words, but what is communicated is not at all common because if it were, there would be nothing to communicate.

In other words, the speaker uses common words to speak about personal things (facts, experiences, feelings), which are uncommon for two reasons: because they are related to personal experience and because this experience must be relevant in some way for it to be worthy of first being remembered and then communicated.

(We do not communicate everything that happens to us, not least because, for the most part, we do not even remember things that are not emotionally relevant).

The words, which are common, and experiences, which are special, are therefore objectively contradictory: words, in fact, must be common in order to be successfully exchanged within the community, while experiences are never common at the level of the individual, though they may be at the level of the community (to its elder members or *a priori* experts such as journalists, judges and teachers).

Words are moreover combined according to syntactical laws to create conversations that recount facts.

But the use of syntactical rules also involves applying logical rules in order to create a correct and consequently acceptable conversation (i.e. one that can be communicated).

The concepts are therefore not only common, but also logically calculable. It is precisely this calculability that makes conversations rational and consequently acceptable.

(Propositional logic exists, that is, the logic of phrases: this is the logic identified by Boole, the man who in 1839 created the formula that all of us apply when we speak or use a computer. We should incidentally take note of the following: George Boole created a way for language to be read by the computer around a century before Alan Turing had the idea of creating the *Turing Machine*. Both were English.)

We should note that even when rational fallacies interfere in conversations, those fallacies can be concealed by appealing to an apparent rationality; that is to say, even irrationality must be hidden behind rationality so that it can be exchanged. Rationality is held in such high esteem that everyone must appeal to it even if they do not make use of it.

But let us return to experiences: they exist because they are sentimentally relevant and for all that language can go some way in communicating and processing them, they cannot be processed and it is usually impossible for the person who had those experiences to communicate them through language.

Let us examine the long series of experiences that are brought together in a biography (we should note: only the biographies of great men exist). This series of experiences, which have emotional origins, is transplanted into rational terrain by the narrator precisely because the experiences are being recounted: they are actually subject to the nature of language.

They are sometimes transferred into a conversation that appears to be impartial, but is in fact biased. This is because the character, who usually is dead, is praised or criticised by someone who has an ulterior motive that is political, cultural, religious etc., to ensure the support of that person for an ongoing cause.

However, the rational nature of language destroys the relationship between experience and feeling despite the fact that feeling itself was the cause or effect of the experience.

(We should note that it is difficult to separate and distinguish between causes and effects outside of the rational order of language. After all, a desired effect is often the cause of an action and a different effect from that which is desired can be the cause of another action.)

Virginia clearly understood that language is intentionally misleading, especially the language used in biographies. Jacob does in fact read Carlyle's essay and probably wonders: *"Does History consist of the Biographies of Great Men?"* (Jacob's Room, Oxford University Press 1999, p. 48).

The obvious absurdity of the question, abandoned in the clutter of objects in Jacob's room like an essay draft, leads the reader to think that the story is nevertheless narrated as if it consisted of the biographies of great men.

For this reason, it could be said that Virginia uses language in an unnatural way: she purifies it of its rational nature by preventing that characteristic from being used in narrative passages, descriptions and explanations, and restoring the link between experience and feeling, which is destroyed by language itself.

Virginia eliminates rational discourse because it is intentionally misleading and for the same reason she even removes spoken language, the conversation. And if there is any conversation, it is trivial.

The psychological aspect

Language exists, of course, for the purpose of communicating and is well adapted for communicating news, but not for communicating experiences, as indicated above.

Has it been, and will it always be, subject to this limitation?

In my opinion, this limitation emerges when language is used rationally and philosophically.

Returning once again to our origins, we can note that philosophy was born and myth concurrently fell into decline in the Greek cultural area during the sixth and fifth centuries BC. In other words, a new way of representing the universe began to replace the traditional way, at least as far as the cultural *elite* was concerned.

But the word *myth* did not have the meaning that we attribute to it today: Hesiod's *Theogony* (eighth century BC), the great theological reorganisation of the Greek religion, was considered to be a complete explanation of the birth and evolution of the cosmos.

Today, even those who believe Greek myth to be a vehicle of profound truth — as I do — cannot share the viewpoint of Hesiod's contemporaries.

But this concerns us today: The *Theogony* is written in Greek, but this same language is not used in the same way by philosophers and it is therefore necessary to translate it, so to say, in order to communicate the meaning to them. Unfortunately, it is as impossible to translate the language of myth into natural language as it is to translate pictorial language.

Virginia offers her own solution to the problem, which is of great artistic value.

Virginia does not explain — because she is suspicious of explanations — but demonstrates by creating an effect that can be perceived by the senses (optically, acoustically etc.) through her use of language, or rather through language, she evokes emotions that are similar to those evoked by the senses.

Emotions that are completely different from those evoked even by outstanding stories.

In fact, the story attributes a type of order to the reality that is represented, which can be defined as "rational".

But the reality that Virginia demonstrates is not irrational, nor is it a chaotic bundle of sensations and emotions given that she substitutes rational order with another type of order, which we can call "emotional".

It is not, however, possible to rediscover a link between the two types of order that leads from one to the other and vice versa, not even that rather complex link that exists between a natural language and another language, which needs to be translated.

This is due to the fact that feeling unites whilst reason divides. The former therefore produces a united reality (holistic), whereas the other produces a divided reality (reductionist).

It might also be possible to understand this phenomenon by reflecting on the nature of Boole's algebra, but it is immensely easier and more fulfilling to understand it by reading Virginia's texts.

We have observed that Virginia's novels do not have plots, but do feature topics; we will now analyse the psychological aspect of these novels.

In my opinion, nothing interested Virginia longer or more deeply than sexual-mental difference i.e. the difference between a female and a male psyche. In a certain sense, this is the main topic of her texts without a story.

The definition of this difference is precisely what was discussed at the beginning of this book: the female psyche organises reality according to feelings (the value and giving field) whereas the male psyche organises reality according to rationality (the price and exchange field). But, despite having already written several thousand words so far, I have not demonstrated this difference to my readers and am unable to do so because language does not transfer an experience, only its rational representation. In other words, you need to have conscious experience of a feeling psyche and a rational psyche to understand the meaning of the words *feeling* and *rationality.* It is *awareness* that allows us to differentiate between them given that all of us inevitably have unconscious experience of feeling or rational psyches.

That being said, what does Virginia do instead of explaining? She exhibits the male psyches and female psyches through language, but deprives that language of its mystifying poison: rationality.

Rationality is removed in the ways, which have already been demonstrated: the elimination of the plot, the elimination of conversations and, finally, the elimination of every form of completeness (personalities, sense, conclusion, explanation). This is because a preferable form of completeness is thus created, which for Virginia is reality.

After all, history does not actually consist of the biographies of great men, nor does the novel consist of the biographies of the protagonists.

But the warm rain of sensations and feelings brings the timeless role of myth back to life, gleaming like a leaping dolphin: male and female; mother and children; father and children; brother and sister; family, the sacred place.

Once she has established the difference between a female and male psyche, Virginia shows that the sex of the mind does not necessarily correspond to that of the body. In other words: male minds exist in female bodies and vice versa.

Such a phenomenon, which occasionally coincides with homosexuality, must not, however, be confused with it (homosexuality, which Virginia tactfully hints at, was as relevant then as it is now). In fact, a psyche is either male or female *a priori* and is not a choice that can be altered, but sexual preferences are even more and are as unquestionable as tastes in food.

Miss Kilman and Lady Bruton (*Mrs Dalloway)* together with Peggy Pargiter (*The Years)* are examples of a male psyche in a female body; William Dodge (*Between the Acts)* exemplifies the reverse combination.

Miss Kilman and Lady Bruton are the rivals of Clarissa Dalloway, an unforgettable woman; Peggy Pargiter is the doting rival of Aunt Eleanor, the female rock at the heart of the Pargiter family; William Dodge is the rival of Giles Oliver, a rather violent man.

We can therefore assume that a matching mental and physical sex is likely, but anyone who has a direct interest in this phenomenon should analyse it more closely given that the exceptions are frequent, interesting, vital and even unconscious

All in all, it seems incorrect to refer to bodies and psyches using the same adjective (male/female). A possible solution would be to define psyches differently e.g. feeling and rational.

But this would be even more incorrect given that it is the psyche itself that determines sex, not the body.

The adjective that qualifies physical sex should therefore be changed instead, but this would be ridiculous and would confuse many people, including electricians who use "male/female" connectors in good faith.

We must therefore accept this ambiguity of language: it is certainly not the only one.

Virginia's female characters are viewed in a good light, but there are some negatives.

The noteworthy female characters are Mrs Dalloway; Mrs Ramsay (*To the Lighthouse)*; Eleanor Pargiter (*The* Years); Lucy Swithin and Isa Oliver *(Between the Acts)*.

Lily Briscoe (*To the* Lighthouse) and Miss la Trobe (*Between the* Acts) — both artists, the former a painter, the latter a comedy writer — must be mentioned separately because they are female figures who are solitary in their personal life, but nevertheless still carry out the typically female unifying function. Lily Briscoe only occasionally offers her services to other people, thanks to the example and influence of Mrs Ramsay, but puts enormous effort into it when she does by blending diverse pictorial elements together in one image (Vanessa, Virginia's beloved sister, was a painter). Miss La Trobe's project is truly ambitious and she carries it out with modest means: she brings a group of villagers together to form an amateur theatre company and unexpectedly makes actors out of even the middle-class members of the audience who have come to watch the play that she has organised and directed. That is not all: she blends the backdrop with the surrounding landscape (pond, wood and hills with their own life of air, earth and water). She also blends the past with the present and an unknown future in which, perhaps, her play will be better understood: for the time being it only arouses perplexity and has barely any effect on the audience members, who rush out to return to their daily lives as it ends. In Miss la

Trobe, it is easy to recognise Virginia herself, at end of her book and her life.

The male characters are clouded in criticism, but there are glimpses of light.

The noteworthy male characters are: Jacob *(Jacob's Room)*; Peter Walsh and Septimus Warren Smith (*Mrs* Dalloway) — the former corresponds emotionally to Clarissa and there is an existential mental correspondence between the latter and Clarissa; Mr Ramsay (*To the Lighthouse)*; Bartholomew Oliver (*Between the* Acts).

We nevertheless collect fragments of both the main and minor characters, but these are not "just fragments" given that there is a reality to these that does not exist on the whole.

She is fully aware that the two psyches, female and male, are meant to work together and complete each other. They do indeed work together, but incorrectly (perhaps) at this point in time, especially in public life.

The "present" is probably just a breath in the long life of men, a breath that does, however, last as long as the story. There are reasons to believe that the psyches "previously" worked together differently and that there was a different relationship between female psyche and male psyche.

But this might be just another image of the perfect Garden of Eden and maybe the working together of the psyches is not a recalled memory, but rather a desidered aim.

There is therefore a feeling of acceptance, almost of affection for her male characters, even when they behave in an unacceptable and incomprehensible way.

What is truly incomprehensible and disgusting is the groundless exercise of violence by men, which manifests itself in brief, unexpected episodes of brutality towards animals.

And this is the reason for which Virginia, at the end of her marvellous argument that has neither head nor tail, sends a guinea to the solicitor out of friendship, with no conditions attached, having explained over tens of pages that the guinea could be put to better use.

We thus realise that Virginia's comprehensive psyche cannot be restricted by the rational "principle of non-contradiction" and that this characteristic, the celebrated flaw of male vulgarity, is precisely what allows her to break free from coherence and therefore from the rules, as well as giving her the ability to understand everyone.

The language is extraordinarily rich with metaphors and often consists of brief phrases juxtaposed with one another and separated by *full stops* and *commas.* This is another homage to the fragmentation of the senses, the discontinuity of mental images, the alternation of often contrasting feelings. All of these factors are smoothed out by the obligatory rationality of a story whose sentences are structured by syntactical subordination and end in *fixed points*.

It is now possible to make a link between *Three Guineas* and the novels.

In the first essay, Virginia speaks about the relationships between Outsiders and Society and concludes that the process of exclusion, which has thus far been endured, could now be appropriated by the excluded if they make use of a new awareness.

But social alienation does not extend to the private dimension, where real life takes place and a new language is required, or perhaps simply the rediscovery of an ancient language of the heart. This language is rediscovered in Virginia's novels with clarity and unparalleled originality.

The language used in *Three Guineas* clearly differs from that used in the novels, but does not contradict them. In fact, what Virginia teases out over the course of two-hundred pages is rationality itself.

CHAPTER FOUR

THE ENGLISH LANGUAGE

Virginia wrote in the English language, her mother tongue.

I will therefore analyse the psychological characteristics of the English language using the Italian language (my mother tongue) as a reference point.

Even if I will not explicitly say so, every characteristic that I observe and mention is therefore understood to distinguish the English language from the Italian language in a psychological sense.

Furthermore, I believe that the psychological characteristics of the Italian language are similar to those of the other main continental languages and that the differences between continental legal systems (civil law) and the English system (common law) stem from these similarities. I also believe that this is why there is a contrast between continental and British philsophies. I will, however, only briefly outline these hypotheses as it is beyond the scope of this book to go into more detail.

I therefore postulate that you can talk about the psychology of a language, which consists of psychological premises that only have an influence on mother tongue users. It follows that some psychological premises are directly transferred from the mother tongue to the individual before it is even possible to criticise them.

In other words, the psychological effects of the language provide an initial supply of pre-judgements that then enable the user to form judgements (e.g. deciding what is desirable and what is not). The term "pre-judgement" means: a pre-formed judgement adopted by the individual and accepted without question insomuch as it forms the foundation for his or her capacity for critical assessment. Linguistic pre-judgement is therefore no different in nature to any other pre-judgement, but is of a superior quality, as we will see.

Linguistic pre-judgements retain this superior quality even when they are mutually opposed, given that one is never inherently superior to the other but can only be more suitable in a given situation.

Chomsky claims that language is as much a part of the human organism as our legs.

With this in mind, we can say that we do not teach children to speak, just as we do not teach them to walk: they will inevitably speak and walk if they are part of a normal human environment.

Even though all humans walk in the same way, they do not, however, all have the same prejudices. In light of my hypothesis regarding the psychological influence of language, it therefore appears to be difficult to separate nature from nurture.

This approach might have been appreciated by Virginia given that she invited readers to accept the difference between men and women without getting lost in endless questions about the causes.

Incidentally, I observe that this difference does not enjoy a good reputation today because it is held that the principal of equal rights should be based on some form of essential natural identity (despite the fact that every religion and myth talks about natural difference). But the difference exists and it is indeed true that male science-fiction writers include female characteristics in their descriptions of aliens, whilst female authors include male characteristics. So there are aliens amongst us, or rather *Outsiders* to use Virginia's words, given that *Outsiders* automatically propagate their own counterparts.

I will now list the psychological characteristics of the English language:

1) A particular concreteness: objects are preferred to concepts.
2) Constant reference to the speaker's subjectivity: it is in fact a language with identifiable speakers rather than impersonal speakers. Verbs are conjugated according to the speaker and even feelings and sensations relate to the speaker rather than an objective observer.
3) Putting traditional words to new uses.
4) Identifying objects according to their function and connections rather than their appearance.
5) Simple grammar, and in particular, syntax with barely any structure.

But how do the above characteristics constitute a set of values that are in reality inseparable and represent in turn the psychological outcome of the language? I will now consider that question:

1. Rather than discussing concepts that group objects together, it is preferable to discuss objects that are archetypal or in some way representative (a prototype, sample etc.). This is the same psychological option that exists in common law, under which a sentence is justified by referring to a previous sentence rather than an abstract norm (a law). An "unknown" object is thus identified by making reference to a known object. The preposition *like* has a key function in the language. In this sense, things do not belong to a concept, but rather seem to be similar to other known things because the person has previous experience of them. I should point out that this point of view continuously links the present to the past so that everything is neither completely new nor completely old and also indicates a tendency towards gradual change, which seems "conservative" in the eyes of continental Europeans.

A common introductory phrase is *as a matter of fact,* which has a "concrete" as opposed to a "conceptual" meaning and is followed by concrete facts. Concrete facts are, moreover, ingrained in the language, the words of which are often onomatopoeic (a word whose sound reproduces the sound that it defines). The word therefore concretely demonstrates its meaning rather than symbolically representing it. The literal Italian translation of *it is likely* is "è probabile" (it is probable), but "è verosimile" (it is plausible) might be a more accurate translation. The conceptual nature of the word "vero" (true) is, however, absent in the word *likely,* which could be translated as follows: "the speaker believes that the event he/she is speaking about (which is clearly not well-known) is similar to events that have repeatedly unfolded in the same way in the past", as the short Latin phrase goes *id quod plerumque accidit*: "what most often happens" (under the same circumstances). This digression serves to make it absolutely clear that the meanings at the heart of the English language can only be translated into Italian using awkward circumlocutions because the two languages contain different pre-judgements. Clearly no translator can work in this manner as that would destroy the meaning of the text. He/she would also be translating into modern-day Italian, which involves attributing different pre-judgements to the translation from those that formed the *background* of the original text. The same thing would happen when mother-tongue Italian speakers compare the translation to the original text or to the English language in general: they cannot alter their own *background* just as they cannot change their own sex, so the English language remains even more persistently foreign since they do not understand its origin; this is a fascinating foreignness, like the foreignness of a woman to a man.

2. The language is constructed to express a clear point of view: not *what we talk about,* but rather *how it appears to the person speaking,* in relation to their senses (specifying which sense organ is concerned) and emotions. Even verbs express the speaker's point of view and thus their intentions and whether they are instigating the action or being subjected to the circumstances. It is a language that expresses viewpoints rather than truths or lies and it is therefore naturally respectful of viewpoints, which can at most be disagreed with.

The phrases *it looks, it sounds, it tastes, it smells, it feels,* which are frequently followed by *like,* indicate how things appear to the eyes, sound to the ears and are perceived by taste, smell and touch in a similar way to something else that is widely known; 'In Italian, the word "sembra" does not succeed in translating the entirety of these meanings, and in any case tends to refer to a concept, rather than an object.

Verb conjugation does not allude to an objective reality, but always reflects the subject's situation and often their beliefs and expectations:

The past: the speaker specifies whether the action has been completed or has an effect on the present: *I was married for twenty years* (but no longer am)/ *I've been married for twenty years* (and still am).

The speaker specifies whether the action was short-lived, started in the past and is still ongoing, or happened frequently: *I sold my car/ I have been selling cars for one year/ I used to sell cars*.

The present: the speaker specifies whether the action is taking place or happens frequently: *I'm studying English (now)/ I study English.*

The future: *I'm studying English tomorrow* (I will definitely study English tomorrow); *I'm going to study English tomorrow* (I have the intention of studying English tomorrow); *I'm going to open the English book* (I am about to open the English book); now *I'll destroy the English book* (I will now destroy the English book); *the English course starts tomorrow* (the English course is scheduled to start tomorrow); *English will always be very important.* The recounted fact is only unconnected to the speaker's will in the final two examples.

3. Respect for individuals' points of view and feelings implies paying attention to the words that were *originally* used to express them, taking both *the individual's origin* and *the language's origin* into account. In short: some words have a wider meaning and a greater value as they represent the earliest meanings, which are thus fundamental. These words are the basis for the formation of successive meanings, which are linked to the old ones via metaphorical bridges. Anything that has the same role can certainly have the same name. It follows that one word usually

has a plurality of meanings that are connected by metaphorical bridges and bring environments and different periods together. This is also why the past is alive. I should point out that the landscape is protected (this could also be done better in England, but is, however, much more effective than in Italy) purely out of respect for those whose feelings are associated with it.

There are far too many examples of this, a handful of which can be found on every page of the dictionary. It is sufficient here to highlight the fact that all of the English technical IT words have been absorbed into the Italian language and remain foreign for now, but are actually normal non-technical words in the English language. In the general stores of the Far West, *software* referred to soft goods (e.g. fabrics) and hardware referred to hard goods (e.g. tools). These humble words have really taken off! If information technology had been developed in Italy, we would have created numerous pretentious words, possibly derived from ancient Greek, like technical medical terms are.

4. It is a consequence of what has just been said that the (variable) form of things matters little, but the (long-lasting) function that these things carry out to respond to long-established needs counts greatly. This is once again why the past is alive (rather than being resurrected or surviving).

The shuttle was originally a component in the mechanical textile loom that moved the thread forwards and backwards; it then became any means of transport that moves in alternate directions between two destinations; finally, it became a spaceship designed to supply orbital stations.

5. The acclaimed grammatical simplicity of the English language is connected to the fact that it is essentially a spoken language: it is so well known that this need not dwelled upon. The written form of the language is derived from the spoken form. The contrary occurred (and perhaps still occurs) with Italian, which is why the language has noble founding fathers (Dante, Manzoni). Fortunately, English is a language with no founding fathers, but many adoring children. Its simple grammar requires strict constructions to allow grammar to be identified through the positioning of phrases.

Phrases start with a subject, followed by a verb; adjectives (and nouns if they can act as adjectives) precede the nouns to which they refer.

But that is not all. The same words can often play different roles in the phrase (usually not the same phrase): noun, verb, adjective. For example, *the bank* refers to the place; to bank means "to deposit money"; bank holidays are official and legal public holidays. It should be noted that *holiday* means "day of celebration" and originally meant "day to be observed", derived from *holy* and *day,* but when *bank* precedes *holiday,* it becomes an adjective and means "day of celebration for the banks" i.e. a day on which the banks are closed. In conclusion, a day dedicated to civil or religious festivities (a "national holiday" in Italy) is concretely defined as a "day in which the banks are closed": this is a good example of concreteness, which *sounds like a profanity* to our ears.

This fluidity in a word's role combined with the various meanings of words leads to a particular outcome: in order to understand a phrase, you need to be familiar with the context i.e. who said (or wrote) it and in what circumstances. In other words, the phrase ceases to be the only unit of meaning in a conversation and only means anything when the person who produced it and whose point of view it reflects, is present.

Re-reading the five points above, it seems that I have consistently said the same thing and only one thing.

But what is it? It might be better to avoid the constraints of a definition given that the English language loves to *escape.* After all, the practice of *spelling,* which involves "pronouncing the letters of a word one by one in order to indicate how a word is spelt", emerged because the English language has a tendency to elude the written form, like a bird the cage.

In my opinion, all that need be noted is that the English language as a whole tends to transfer a point of view to its users that has great similarities with the one proposed by Virginia in her text, which can be summarised as follows:

1) The concreteness that can be obtained through perceptible objects; the reduction of concepts and logical reasoning;
2) The presentation of subjective points of view;
3) The use of metaphors and images;
4) The use of words that are loaded with long-established meanings and thus with feeling;
5) The de-structured syntax of the spoken language.

In other words, Virginia's text reinforces the psychological premises that are naturally possessed by the English language and makes them clear. It also embodies prejudices, so to say.

But then again, if Virginia is also expressing the viewpoints of "Outsiders", this means that English might be more suited to the nature of Outsiders than the continental languages are.

It might not be coincidental that there have been many female writers whose mother-tongue is English, even if British society did not favour female writers any more than continental societies, and perhaps favoured them to an even lesser degree.

Henry James (1843-1916) observed that many British novelists were women and that this phenomenon could not be seen to the same extent in the literature of other countries. But it would be more correct to say: in literature written in other languages.

This is why I believe that English is a "female language", perhaps not the only female language, but certainly the main one. I believe that this point is worthy of being developed by whoever has the ability to do so and wishes to rebel against the current trend of seeing in the two sexes a commonality of nature.

It can be hoped that this English language, which is allergic to ideology, will help to cure the great evils that ideology has caused, particularly in the twentieth century, the short and bloodthirsty century.

Printed in July 2017
by Youcanprint *Self-Publishing*